I'll Never
Forget
the Love That
I Shared
with You

I'll Never Forget the Love That I Shared with You

A collection of poems
Edited by Robin Andrews

Blue Mountain Press ®

Boulder, Colorado

Library of Congress Catalog Card Number: 91-73569
ISBN: 0-88396-349-3

ACKNOWLEDGMENTS appear on page 62.

 design on book cover is registered in
U.S. Patent and Trademark Office.

Manufactured in the United States of America
First Printing: September, 1991

Blue Mountain Press ®

P.O. Box 4549, Boulder, Colorado 80306

CONTENTS

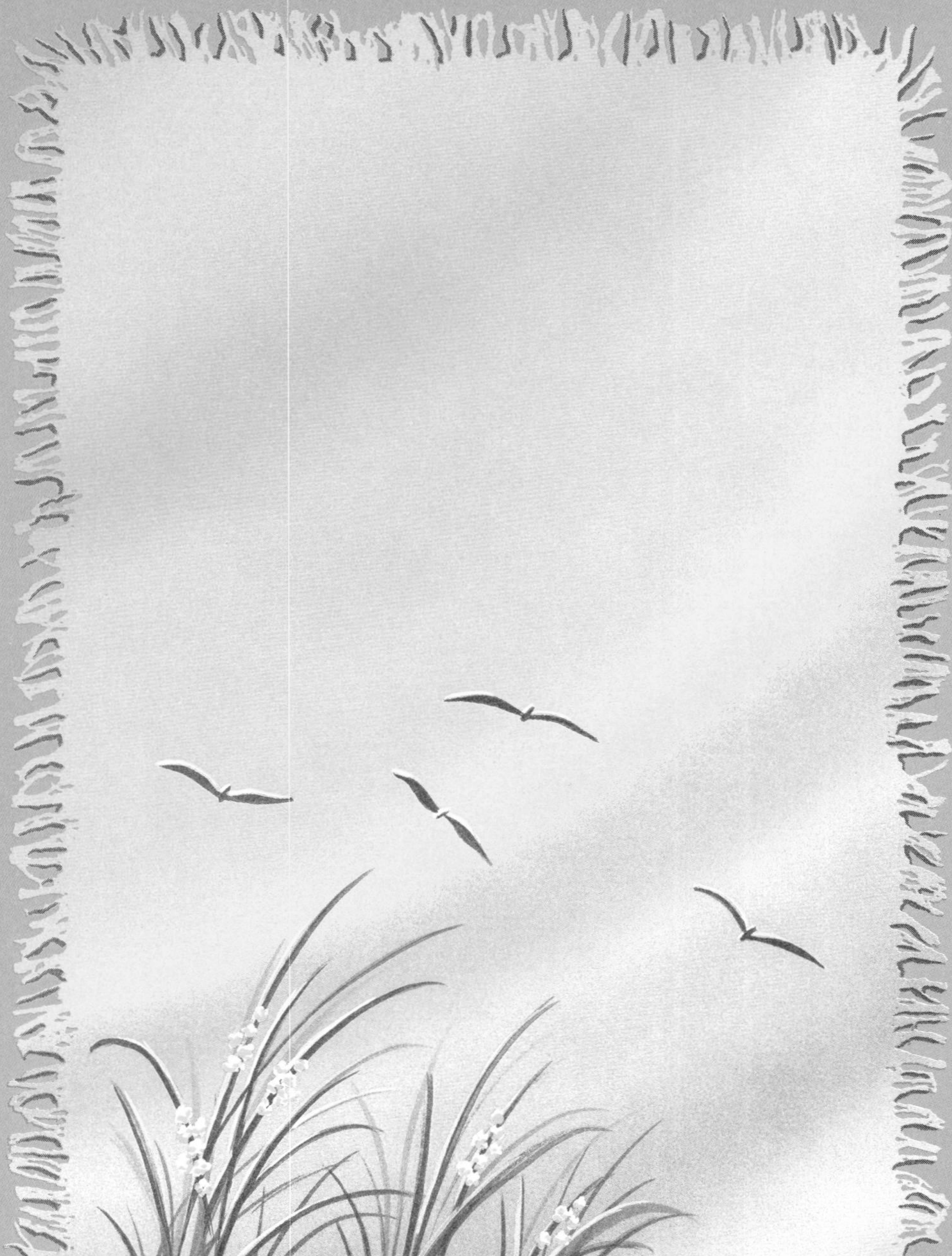

I'll Never Forget the Love
That I Shared with You

I know that someday I'll get
used to the fact that we're
                    not together anymore.
And that maybe we won't be . . .
                    ever again.

Time will tell.
In the meantime, though,
you may be away from my arms,
but you will never be
                    very far from my heart.

I know the love will never leave.
There are too many memories;
there were so many precious moments
    and wonderful times
                    to ever try to forget . . .

And I just want you to know
that I will remember,
        for the rest of my days,
how you helped me find
some happiness and some truths and
    how you opened some beautiful doors.

        I'll never forget
        how good it was
        to share a part of my life
                    with yours.

                                        —Collin McCarty

You'll Always Be a Special Part of Me

Now that we've been apart for a while
and had a chance to sort out our thoughts,
I feel I am ready to express myself to you
in a way I was not able to before.
At the time, I knew we both just
needed some time alone,
and although it was hard for me
to watch you turn and leave,
I knew I couldn't run after you.
There are so many things I need you
to know, though.

Please believe me when I say
that your happiness is very important to me.
I hope that I did not hurt you
with any words spoken in frustration
or any actions during our final days together.
You touched my life in a very special way
and left a warm mark in my heart
that no one will ever be able to take away.
I still dream about you,
remembering moments we spent with friends
    or alone,
sometimes talking and laughing over daily events,
and other times just staying quietly
    next to each other,
enjoying the peace that seemed to surround us.
I hold these memories close to my heart,
and I hope that when you think of me,
you remember me as I remember you —
    with love.

—Chris Ardis

Let's Never Let Go
of What We Shared

I don't ever want us to let go
of each other.
Maybe our paths will go
in separate directions,
but that won't change the bond
we share and what's in our hearts.

No matter where I am
or what I am doing,
when you come to mind
a smile comes to my face
and a warmth settles in my heart.

The day you and I met
will always be cherished.
We've grown together,
done a lot together,
and no matter what,
we will always care
about each other.

I often struggle to say how I feel,
but I hope we never let go
of what we shared,
because whether it's across the miles
or just a short distance,
you are and will always be
a part of my life and me.

—Betsy Gurganus

I'll Always Care About You

I always thought that
loving someone was enough.
I truly believed that
if two people cared deeply,
nothing could ever
come between them.
But we both know this
isn't always true;
the obstacles we faced
became overwhelming.
I know how hard you tried;
we both did.
But all the patience
and time in the world
couldn't change
what we faced.

It has been said that,
if you really love someone,
you must be willing
to let them go.
As difficult as it was,
this was what we chose.
But I want you to know that
I don't regret one moment
we shared.
Always remember that
wherever life takes us separately,
there will be
a special love between us
forever linking our hearts together.

—Diane Hayes Beers

Even though we're not together anymore,
I want to wish you happiness.
I still care for you,
and I still love you
just as I always have.

Your love was once
a very important part of my life,
and it still is.
No matter what has happened,
nothing has changed the way
I feel about you,
and nothing will ever change
the love we once shared.
I will never forget that love,
and I will never regret it,
just as I will never forget you.
You will remain in my heart forever.
I am glad that we are still friends;
that is very special to me.
And just because we are no longer in love,
the love I feel has not changed.
No matter where our lives lead us,
you will be a part of me forever.

—Amy Michele Shockey

You Are Still
One of the Special People
in My Life

There are cherished people
whom we carry in our hearts
wherever we go in life.
We may spend a lot of time
together,
getting to know each other
and sharing each other's lives,
then have to move on
to other places.
But no matter where we go,
we always remember
the special people
who touched our lives.

We always remember
the special people
who loved us and helped us
learn more about ourselves;
the people who stayed by us
when we had to face difficult times,
and with whom we felt safe enough
to reveal our true selves;
the special people
we dreamed and planned
great futures with,
who accepted us as we were
and encouraged us to become
all that we wanted to be.

—Donna Levine

I think about you so much
I wonder if you are having fun
I wonder if you are happy
I wonder if you are feeling well
Though we don't see each other
   very often
you are with me
in my thoughts

—Susan Polis Schutz

My Memories of
the Love We Shared
Will Be with Me Forever

When the time came for us
to say good-bye,
I was filled with sadness,
knowing that I would never again
feel your touch
or look into your eyes.
My mind was filled with
so many thoughts
that were never spoken
and never will be.

We had to go our separate ways,
but I have no regrets.
I would not give up the time
we had together,
nor erase the memories,
for these are things that last
through a lifetime.

And even though the memories
may fade as time goes by,
there will always be something,
somewhere, to spark a memory anew.
For this I am thankful.
I wish for you the best
that life has to offer.
I hope you find that special
happiness that I so wanted
for you and me.
And as each day passes,
remember that you have a friend
somewhere who loves you,
and that a part of me
will be yours forever.

—Frances D. Mathews

I Still Think of You

I know it was right for us
to go our separate ways;
we had gone as far
    as we could go together.
But even though I know
it had to be this way,
I still miss the laughter,
    the happy times,
and the magic of our memories.
I still miss you.

You gave me so much
in the time we had.
You gave me the courage
to step out and be myself.
You made me laugh when
I got too absorbed in my worries.
You challenged me to stretch
    my horizons,
to open my mind, to live completely.
You taught me what it means
to give to another person
with everything I am,
because that is how you gave to me.

—Donna Taylor

There Are Still Times When
I Wish We Could Give
Our Love One More Chance

I tell myself the love is gone,
but in the same breath a little voice
whispers it's still there.
I tell myself I don't miss you,
but every day, everywhere,
I look for you.
I tell myself it wasn't meant to be,
but in remembering how good it was,
I find that difficult to believe.
I tell myself I don't really care,
while the sound of your voice
makes my heart leap.

I tell myself love will come again,
yet at the same time I wonder
whom you will be loving then.
I tell myself it's over,
but my heart refuses to accept that.
I tell myself to forget you,
and I try, I really try,
but you make it hard to do
by staying on my mind.
I tell myself that no one
is worth this much pain,
but then no one has given me
so much happiness.
I tell myself life isn't
so bad without you,
even as I wish you were
in my life again.

—Nancye Sims

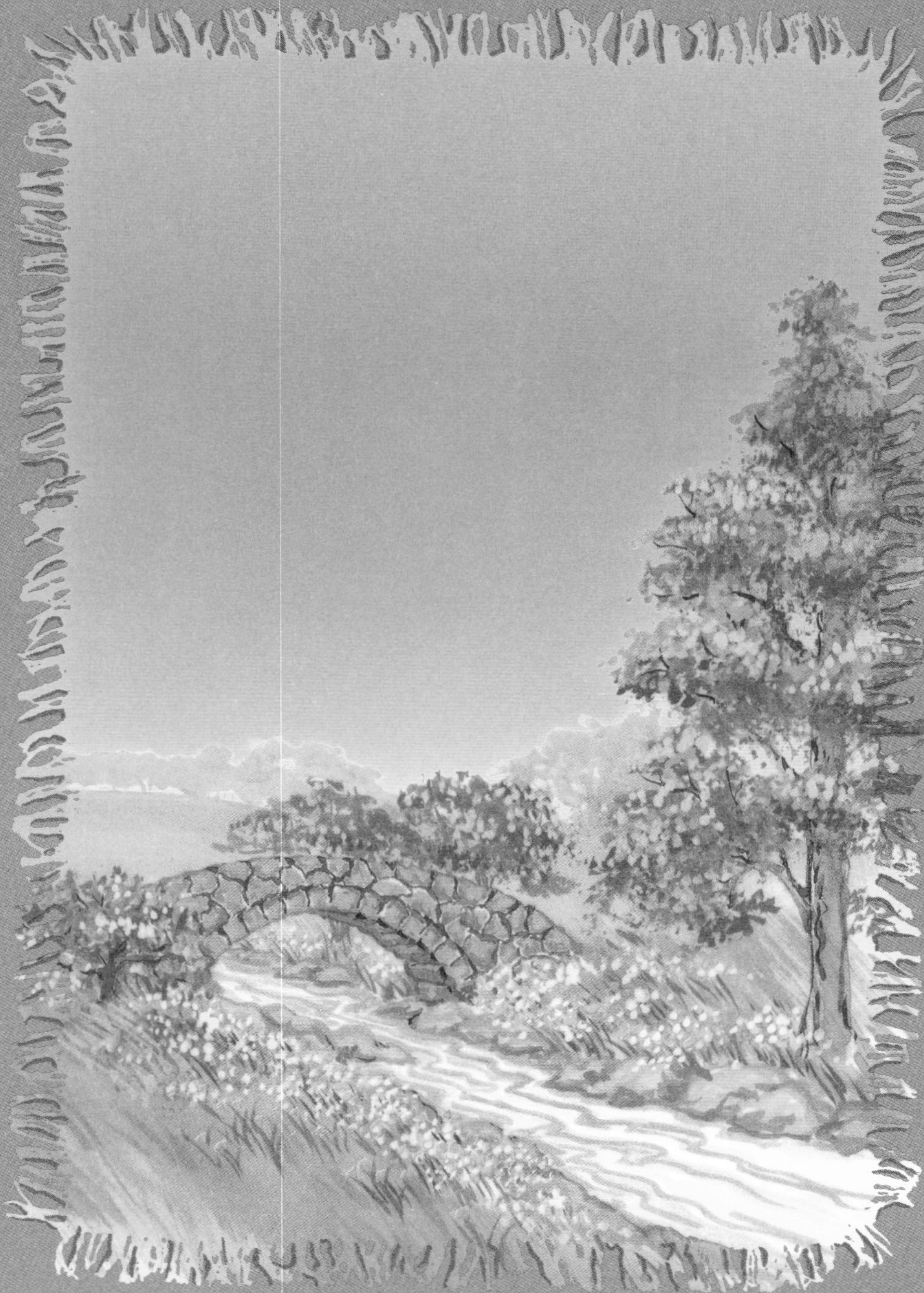

I Really Miss You Sometimes

When you've cared about someone
as much as I did about you,
being apart
   is a hard thing
      to get used to.

I thought I'd handle it just fine . . .
      and that I'd be happy
just to keep you on my mind.
But it isn't always that easy.

Sometimes the one thing that would
please me the most . . . is simply
      seeing you.

   I knew that I'd miss you.

      I just didn't know
         I'd miss you
            as much as I do.

—Alin Austin

Every now and then,
I think about you
and the world
we once shared together.

I don't regret our decision
to go in different directions;
what I do regret
is not getting the chance
to have met you
later in my life,
because I have a feeling
things would have been
different for us both.

We may not share our lives
together anymore,
but I hope you're doing well
and getting the things
you want from life.
You will always be
a part of my thoughts,
which is another way of saying
that I'll always think
you're special.

—Terry Everton

No matter where
or when I ramble
no matter what
may be my goal
when I think of you
and nights gone by, Love
I feel a warmth
deep in my soul

—Hoyt Axton

The People We Love Most
Are Forever in Our Hearts

Some people touch our lives
and become a part of us forever.
Even when they are no longer with us,
we still think of them as being close.
We feel their warmth, and remember
special things they said and did,
and times we shared.

And sometimes, we hurt because
they aren't with us; we miss them
so intensely and think of things
we wish we'd said.
But we can find strength
in the impact they made
on our lives; we are so much richer
for our association with them.
We can smile, and celebrate
the realization that love
is unlimited by distance or time,
and that our hearts will forever hold
the people who fill our thoughts.

—Shelby Lewis Jones

Although We're Not Together Anymore, I Am Thinking of You and Wishing You Happiness

As I sit here so far away from you,
   remembering our love from so long ago,
I think about how much I loved you then.
The feelings I had for you never changed,
   but I did.
And tonight,
wherever you are,
whatever you are doing,
I wish I could just tell you that
   I'm thinking about you.
I want you to be happy,
and I hope that someday
you will find someone who will
   love you
as much as I once did.

—Glenda Willm

The memories of you and me
don't cause me pain anymore
Certain songs still bring you to mind
but gently and without tears
Time works its magic
and with time comes strength
and wisdom and peace
I've become strong enough to stand alone
and it's a wondrous feeling
I've become wise enough to realize
that what we shared was precious
and it was ours alone
I'm content with the awareness
that you and I did have our time together
and it cannot be taken from us
And now, alone, strong, and wise
I can bring to mind over and over
our lovely moments, our music, our laughter
The memories make me smile
and feel warm inside
and I know I will return to those times
again and again
Our story would be complete
if you, too, journeyed back in time
to recall now and then
all that made us special.

—Rhoda-Katie Hannan

I Still Remember
the Wonderful Times We Shared

Whenever I think of you,
I can't help but smile
as I remember the wonderful times
we used to share.
I remember how we would
talk for hours
and never run out of things to say,
how we laughed at everything
and cried at nothing,
how we dreamed about the future
and never doubted that someday
all those dreams would come true.

I miss the happy times
we used to share;
I miss having you to confide in
and that special understanding
we shared.
There have been a lot
of changes in our lives since then.
But in spite of the time
and distance that separate us,
I think of you often,
and those memories never fail
to brighten up my day.

—Kathleen McMahan

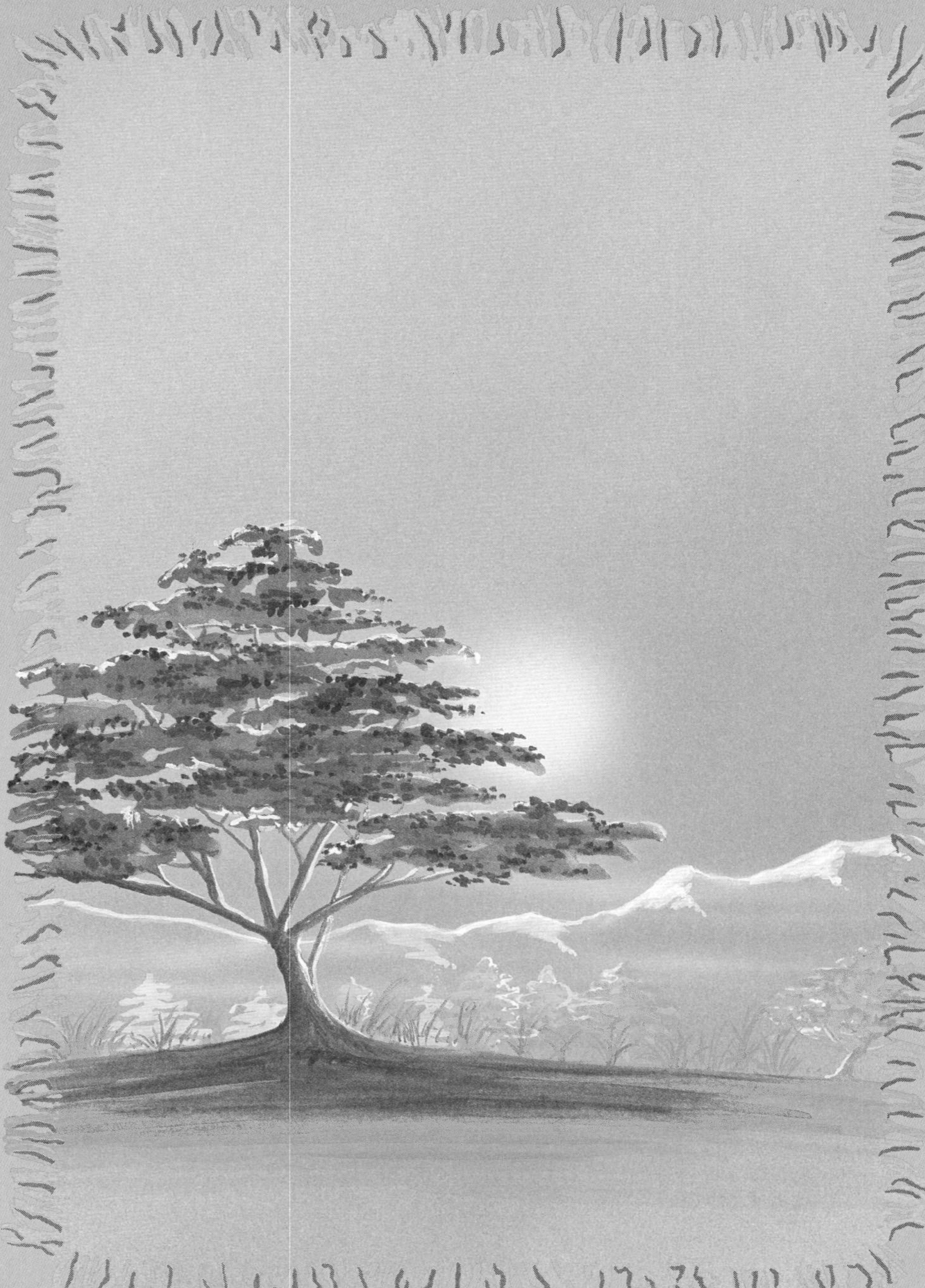

Thank You for Touching My Life

Sometimes people who come into your life
   make changes in you,
because you always take a little
part of them with you into the future.
We are all made up
of little bits and pieces of those
   whose lives touch ours.

I won't ever forget you
or what you meant to my life.
Many times people are brought together
   for a reason.
I believe we met so that we could grow
to become a little more
of the people we were meant to be.
Thank you for helping me become who I am,
for giving of yourself,
and for letting me give
   something back to you.
I wish you all of the best in life
and thank you so very much
   for touching mine.

—Rodger Austin

Even When Two People Say Good-Bye, They Remain in Each Other's Heart

Life is like a journey.
We may be walking along a path
    with someone,
and then come upon a crossroad
where we each must choose
the road that is right
for each of us individually.
At times we may find ourselves
    walking a path alone,
but somewhere along the road
we find new people to walk with,
    to love,
        to grow with,
            to share with.

The path of life has many crossroads,
and at each one it's difficult
to say good-bye
and go our own separate ways,
choosing the direction that is
right for each of us.
But the memory of being together
will always remain,
and there is always the chance
that our paths will cross again.

—Donna Yee

What We Shared Continues to Be Very Special to Me

Our daily togetherness is a thing
of the past,
   but my sweet and special
      feelings for you
         will last
            as long as I live.

If you ever think of us,
I hope with all my heart
that you will remember
   the smiles and the love
and the memories that only we two
   can carry within.

My life will always be
better and more beautiful
because of what you and I shared.

Thank you for the wonderful
memories.
I'll treasure them forever.

—Chris Gallatin

May Life Bring You
Everything You Wish For

I hope that your life is always filled
with the joy of friends and family,
and that each day brings you
the pleasures and deep rewards
of love and friendship.
I hope that your heart is always at peace,
that in unsteady and uncertain times
you will always have something
to hold on to as a source
of comfort and peace
in your thoughts,
your beliefs, and your life.
I hope that your efforts are
always rewarded, and that you
experience the joy of achievement
and always have the excitement
of meaningful challenges.

I hope that you'll always find
the things that matter most to you,
that your responsibilities
will still leave you with
the time and freedom for
the people and activities
that provide your deepest satisfaction.
I hope that the end of every journey
provides a chance for reflection
and appreciation for everyone
who helped you
and for everything you gained
along the way.

—Garry LaFollette

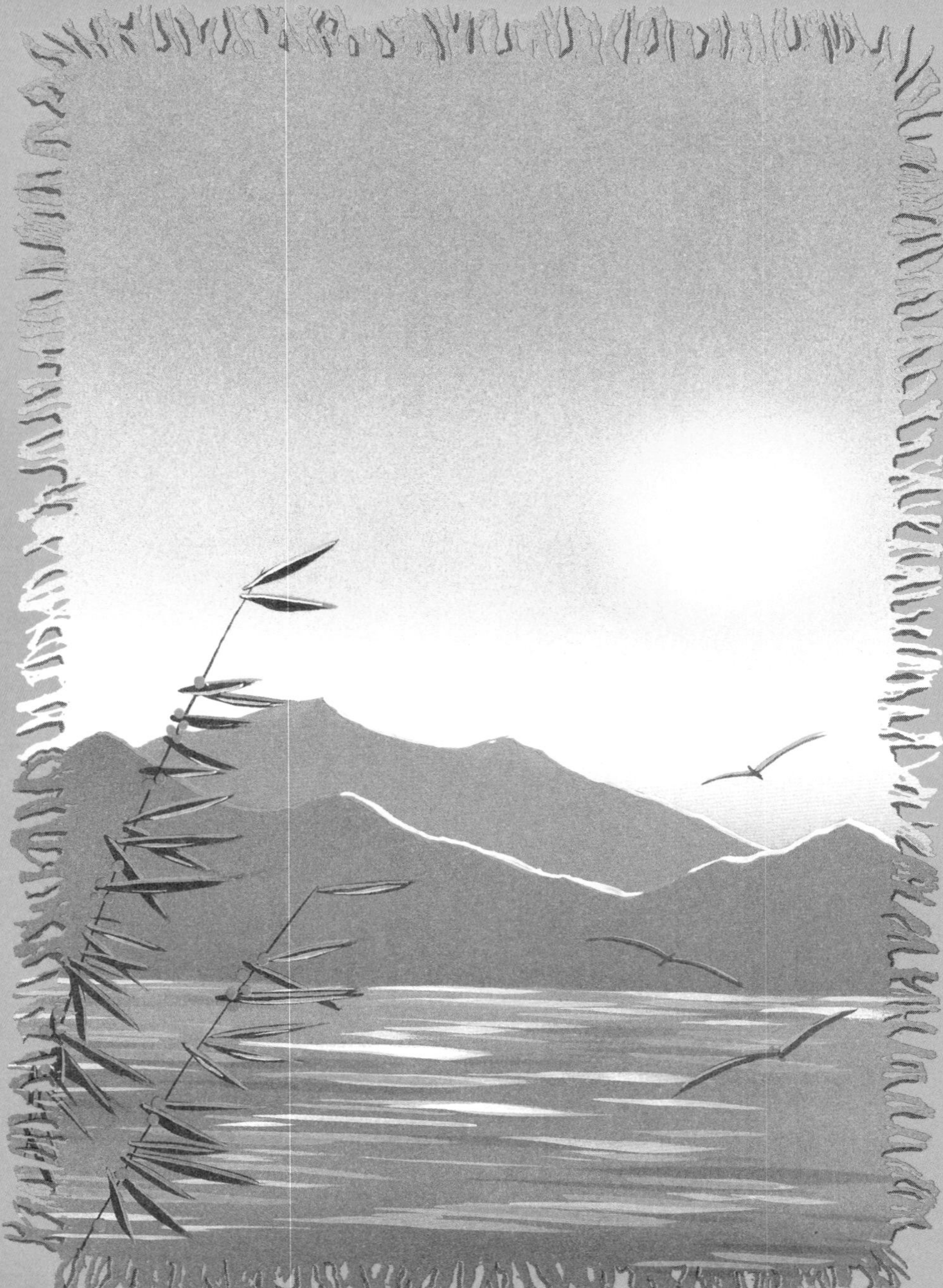

Even though we are no longer
   together,
I want you to know that the
   times we shared
are still very special to me.
In spite of the bad times,
we were and still are very
   fortunate in many ways,
and it's the good times that
   I want us to remember.
Today, I find myself wanting
   so much for you to be happy
and for life to be good to you.
I hope you'll continue to take
   good care of yourself.

—Charles E. Gries

The Past Is Past, but Tomorrow Will Last Forever

Our lives have so many
backward glances in them,
don't they . . .
We think back to how things
were and how things might
have been . . .

There's nothing wrong with
thinking back, but it probably is
a mistake to dwell on
    the past "what ifs."
Instead, we should concentrate
on today, on tomorrow,
and on the tomorrows yet to be.

There are a lot of beautiful days
    yet to come.

The past is past . . .
    but tomorrow will last forever.
And I'll never stop hoping that
    each tomorrow
will fill your heart with love
    and laughter,
your days with dreams come true,
    and your life with so much
        happiness to look forward to.

—Laurel Atherton

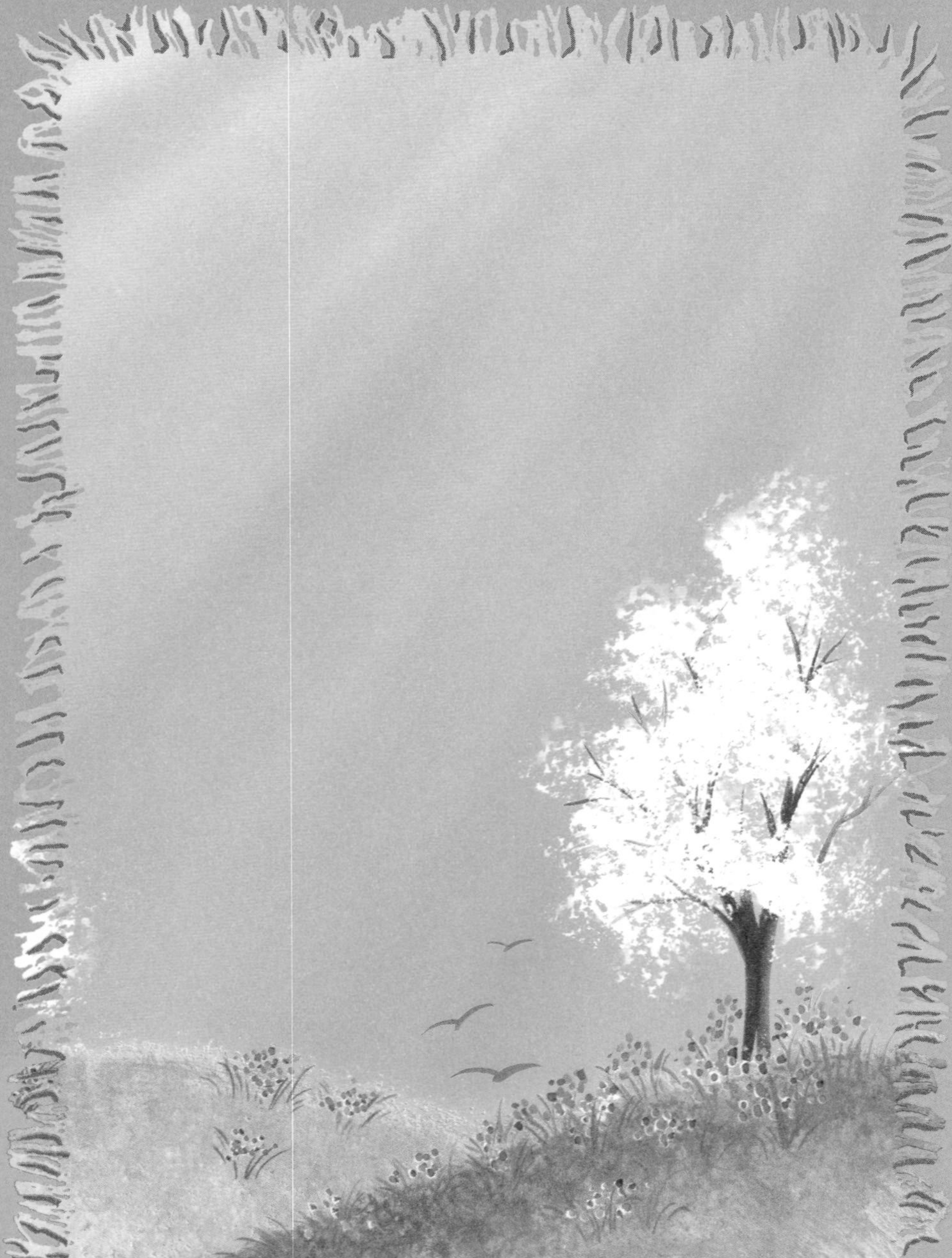

So many times each day
I am reminded of you
I do things that we did together
I hear things that we heard together
I see things that we saw together
So many times each day
I am reminded of you
And at the end of every day
I think of the memories
and I just want to say
thanks

—Susan Polis Schutz

I'll Never Regret
the Part of My Life
I Shared with You

It seems like so very long ago now
that I held you in my arms and my heart.
I often wonder where I would be today
without what we've shared.
We went through a lot of changes
during the course of our relationship,
and I don't regret how I've turned out
because of them.
You initiated some feelings in me
that helped open an entirely new form
of intensity in my life,
and there are times when I still feel you
and your influence.

Why we chose to cross each other's paths
when we did is still a miracle
that I don't completely understand,
but I've learned to accept it
and all that we were led through
because of it.
I guess I just want you to know that
I'm still living the kinds of things
that you taught me.
There are moments when I know
I couldn't make it without what we had. . .
and that's something I can't say
to just anyone.

—Whitney Miles

My thoughts often turn to you.
I wonder what you're doing,
what challenges life
   is offering you,
and if you think about
   our relationship.
It seems hard to believe
that we've both ended up
   in different places,
needing different things,
experiencing different aspects
   of life.
We've shared with one another
deeply and intensely,
and now we're separated,
each dealing with our own life,
living with the memories
   of what's behind us.
But my thoughts turn to you often,
   hoping that you're happy.
No matter how much time goes by,
or even if we don't see
   one another much,
I'll always care about you.

—Sherrie L. Householder

Think about me sometimes . . . okay?
Even though we're not together
   the way we used to be,
it still seems so natural
   and so easy to think of you
and all the good times we shared.

Any hard times we had
seem to fade away so quietly,
but the memories of all the
   smiles and special times
will stay with us
and never disappear.

Guess I just wanted
to say `` hello''
. . . and tell you that
I have one wish
that I wish you'd grant me —
for old-times' sake, today:
   just that I hope you'll
      think about me
         sometimes . . . okay?

—Andrew Tawney

I'll Always Wish These Things for You

Happiness. Deep down within.
Serenity. With each sunrise.
Success. In each facet of your life.
Family. Beside you.
Close and caring friends.
Health. Inside you.

Special memories. Of all the yesterdays.
A bright today. With much to be
    thankful for.
A path. That leads to beautiful
    tomorrows.

Dreams. That do their best to come true.
Appreciation. Of all the
    wonderful things about you.

—Collin McCarty

I don't ever want to forget
the time we shared . . .

My life goes on without you,
   the days pass . . .
But then I have days
   when I think of you,
and the memories bring a smile
   and a little sadness, too.
I don't ever want to forget the
   time we shared.
I was so happy then . . .
the days passed so slowly
   until I would see you again.
I don't want to forget how it felt
   to be so excited about another,
or your gentleness and consideration
   of me.
I especially don't want to forget
how much I wanted to give back
just a little of the happiness
   you gave to me.
It does not matter that we may never
   meet again . . .
it only matters that once there was
   a "you and me."
No matter how brief our time together,
   or what tomorrow may bring,
I wanted you to know that I could
   never forget you.

—Anne Wolfe

Though We're Not Sharing Our Lives Anymore, I'll Still Think of You

Even though our relationship
isn't what it was,
I still consider you my friend,
and I hope life
brings you all the happiness
that you deserve.

You are still an integral part
of my life in so many ways.
I often find myself thinking
about our time together,
and it always makes me feel
happy whenever I do.

I hope that you are well
and that you are discovering
everything you hoped to find.
You still mean a lot to me,
and I'll always remember
the love that we once knew.

—Terry Everton

ACKNOWLEDGMENTS

The following is a partial list of authors whom the publisher especially wishes to thank for permission to reprint their works.

Amy Michele Shockey for "Even though we're not together. . . ." Copyright © 1991 by Amy Michele Shockey. All rights reserved. Reprinted by permission.

Donna Taylor for "I Still Think of You." Copyright © 1991 by Donna Taylor. All rights reserved. Reprinted by permission.

Terry Everton for "Every now and then. . . ." Copyright © 1991 by Terry Everton. All rights reserved. Reprinted by permission.

Hoyt Axton for "No matter where or when I ramble . . . ." From the song, "I Feel a Warmth." Copyright © by Hoyt Axton. All rights reserved. Reprinted by permission.

Shelby Lewis Jones for "The People We Love Most. . . ." Copyright © 1991 by Shelby Lewis Jones. All rights reserved. Reprinted by permission.

Glenda Willm for "Although We're Not Together. . . ." Copyright © 1991 by Glenda Willm. All rights reserved. Reprinted by permission.

Rhoda-Katie Hannan for "The memories of you and me. . . ." Copyright © 1991 by Rhoda-Katie Hannan. All rights reserved. Reprinted by permission.

Kathleen McMahan for "I Still Remember the Wonderful Times. . . ." Copyright © 1991 by Kathleen McMahan. All rights reserved. Reprinted by permission.

Rodger Austin for "Thank You for Touching My Life." Copyright © 1991 by Rodger Austin. All rights reserved. Reprinted by permission.

Whitney Miles for "I'll Never Regret the Part of My Life. . . ." Copyright © 1991 by Whitney Miles. All rights reserved. Reprinted by permission.

A careful effort has been made to trace the ownership of poems used in this anthology in order to obtain permission to reprint copyrighted materials and to give proper credit to the copyright owners. If any error or omission has occurred, it is completely inadvertent, and we would like to make corrections in future editions provided that written notification is made to the publisher:

BLUE MOUNTAIN PRESS, INC., P.O. Box 4549, Boulder, Colorado 80306.